LINE O

A history of firefighting
in Lewes

Bill Young

S.B. Publications

For Margaret Kirkwood,
East Sussex Fire Brigade 1973-1976

First published 1996 by Bill Young
in association with S. B. Publications
c/o 19 Grove Road, Seaford, East Sussex BN25 1TP

ISBN 1 85770 093

Printed by Island Press Ltd.,
3 Cradle Hill Industrial Estate Seaford, East Sussex BN25 3JE
Tel: (01323) 490222 UK

CONTENTS

ACKNOWLEDGMENTS

MANY people helped me in various ways and at various times during the writing of this book. I would particularly like to thank John Bassett, Arthur Bowles, Bob Cairns, Cyril Elphick, Mrs John Geering, Bill Izzard, Ian Lowrie, Neville Mountford, Harold Ovenden, Lillian Puttock, Vince Richardson and Mike Turner. I am especially indebted to Daisy Fisher, who cheerfully deciphered my scrawled handwriting and typed my first draft and to Peter Morphew, lately County Fire Officer, East Sussex Fire Brigade, for his encouragement.

INTRODUCTION

'And it be further enacted, that the said Inspectors shall from Time to Time employ such Number of able-bodied Watch-House Keepers, Sergeants of the Night, Watchmen, Patrols, Streetkeepers and other Persons, as they think sufficient for the proper Protection of the Inhabitants and Houses, and who shall use their utmost Endeavours to prevent any Mischief by Fire. The said Inspectors shall provide and keep up Fire Engines, with Pipes and other Utensils proper for the same . . .

THE above extract from the Lighting and Watching Act of 1830 – an adoptive Act applying to parishes in England and Wales – serves as a reminder that the fire service has featured in the Statute Books for more than 150 years.

Although the history of the fire service in this country can be traced back to the Roman army of occupation, the earliest record of any form of organised fire fighting in Lewes is 1559. It was in that year that the Town Constables disbursed charges 'for men to watche when the grete fyer was yn Westowte'.

This book details the changes and developments of the fire service in Lewes from the sixteenth century to the present day when there are yet more changes in the offing. The fires and incidents which made the headlines are here, as well as the people who dealt with them. In the early years they had to do so with most primitive appliances and without pay. Today they are skilled professionals, dealing with a wide range of complex incidents using modern technology. But still, fire is fire. It takes courage and commitment to face it – and those are qualities the firefighters of Lewes have displayed through the ages, as these pages will show.

1 THE EARLY DAYS

THE history of organised fire fighting goes back almost 2,000 years. In the days of the Roman Republic it was carried out by bands of slaves who were stationed around the walls and gates of the city. The service they provided was not very efficient and, after a disastrous fire, the Emperor Augustus (BC 63 to AD 14) established a corps of fire-fighting Vigiles – from the Latin *virgilia* meaning awake, watchful – who were to protect Rome for the next 500 years.

The Corps of Vigiles, the modern equivalent of which would be the Sapeurs-Pompiers of Paris, a brigade of the French army which operates the fire department of Paris, was not confined to Rome. Some were, in fact, stationed in this country, although it is not certain whether they were performing a fire fighting role or were being used to supplement the army of occupation.

From the early fifth century, when Britain ceased to be a peripheral colony of Rome, Lewes, like many other towns on or near the North Sea and Channel coasts, was burned and pillaged by marauding Danes before King Alfred put a stop to their incursions. No doubt there were fires in plenty but it is not until the Battle of Lewes in 1264 that there is a written record of the town in flames. It was set alight deliberately by Simon de Montfort's victorious rebel army in order to smoke out the remaining supporters of the royalist cause. Blazing arrows were even fired from the castle ramparts on to the Priory of St Pancras, where the defeated king, Henry III, had taken refuge. The fire they started was soon extinguished.

'Most of the private buildings of the town were thatched with straw and kindled into flames with the first wandering spark they caught,' says an account of the battle in *The Chronicle of Walter Hemingford,* written by a Yorkshire monk who died in 1347.

Fire raising for military reasons was one thing, arson another – in the days when wood formed the framework, if not the entire structure, of most buildings. The punishment for it was Draconian, and fitted the crime – the culprit was burned alive.

Another 300 years go by before the next recorded conflagration.

An entry in the Lewes Town Book in 1559 records that Constables John Chatfyld and Thomas Sherman: 'disbursed yn charges . . . for men to watche when the grete fyer was yn Westowte. . .'– Westowte being that part of Lewes outside the West Gate, that is, the area around St Anne's Hill.

Four years previously the Constables had paid out for the 'newe casting of the common bell', a reference to the great town bell 'Gabriel' which today hangs in the old Market Tower in Market Street. It was then hung in the bell loft of the Church of St Nicholas, which stood on the site of the present war memorial. 'Gabriel' was used for a number of purposes, among them to sound the alarm, which is what it undoubtedly did for the 'Westowte' fire. It was still being used as a fire alarm as late as 1842.

From the sixteenth century the management of Lewes was undertaken by a council called the Society of Twelve. Its members were among the wealthier and more influential citizens and they elected officers to carry out various duties. Two Constables were appointed and they were responsible for procuring and maintaining the primitive fire fighting equipment available in those days 'for use by the townsfolk for the common good.' In 1576, according to the Town Book, it consisted of twelve 'lethere bucketes', two great 'eyrne whockes wth chaines vppon them' and two 'greate poles mad ffor the yovse of ffyre if ned Reqvyre wthin the towne'.

This equipment, some pieces of which were so large that several men were required to handle them, was for a number of years the town's sole fire fighting apparatus.

The whereabouts of the first fire station is a matter of conjecture. The introduction to the first Town Book of Lewes suggests it was probably at the Market Hall which was built in 1564 and stood in the middle of the High Street, between Castle Gate and what is now known as St Martin's Lane. Another source places it at the Old Town Hall or Sessions House, which was built in the same year and was also in the middle of the High Street, near the top of Station Street.

There is a brief reference in the Town Book to a fire which swept

OLD TOWN HALL. LEWES. 1761

The old town hall or Sessions House, demolished in 1801, may well have been Lewes's first fire station. It stood in the middle of the High Street, opposite the White Hart Hotel.

through the part of Lewes containing the lands and buildings of the Steward of the Lords of the Castle. Today all that remains of that great estate is a street name – Stewards Lane. The inventory of 1592 lists, among other items: 'x lethere buckettes, xij mattockes & xij shovells of which viij were lost at the fyre at Stewardes Inn'.

For another 100 years Lewes kept and used the same basic fire fighting equipment. It was not until 1680 – fourteen years after the Great Fire of London had destroyed more than 13,000 houses, nearly 100 churches, most of the capital's public buildings and made 100,000 people homeless – that the town acquired its first fire engine.

Among the items handed over in that year by Ralph Richardson to the new Constables were: 'Three ingines, one great and two small'.

These would have been crude wooden contraptions consisting of a wooden cistern on wheels, filled with water from a manual bucket chain. The cistern acted as a reservoir and a hand-operated pump would force the water out of a gooseneck shaped pipe in spurts. By 1690 these engines had been reduced to two in number – 'one great and one small'.

Hoses made of hand stitched leather were invented by Dutchman Jan Van Der Heyden in 1672. They made it possible for the fire fighters to get closer to the fire without endangering their engines and also made it possible to get water on to the flames with more accuracy. These leather hoses needed to be kept soft and pliant with oil and in the Constables' Accounts for 1731 is the entry: 'Paid for oil for the engine pipes 1/-'.

In 1726 'Thomas Pelham of Lewes' gave an engine with two leather pipes to the town and five years later 'Thomas Pelham of Stanmer' gave an engine of smaller size. The Constables Accounts note the payment of 2s 6d 'for writing Mr Pelham's name as donor of ye fire engine'.

These engines were almost certainly made by Richard Newsham, a pearl button maker who, in 1721, patented a new design of manual fire engine. His idea was to arrange the pumping facilities in such a way that as many men as possible could be set to work on the pumping operation. He did so by placing the pump handles along the sides of the machine, rather that at the ends. On his larger engines he also provided treadles in the centre of the engine so that additional men could throw their weight into the pumping rhythm by working with their legs. The pumpers were assisted in their task by long fixed rails on top of the machine which give it the appearance of a four poster bed.

Pumping was hard work and, as there were no paid firefighters, the Constables had to enlist the aid of fit and healthy citizens to carry out this activity. These volunteers also had to haul the engines to the fire or to the place where they were to be tested. How much they received for their toil is listed in the accounts:

1730	Paid the men to drink for getting out and trying the fire engine	2s 6d
1750	Paid for the beer in playing the engines when cleaned	2s 0d
1775	For beer for the men who played the engines	4s 6d
1814	Norman's bill for bread and cheese and beer for working the engines	15s 6d

At regular intervals there are records of payments for maintenance of the engines and other equipment:

1731	For mending the Ingen after the fire	5s 0d
1741	Paid to get the Engines out to see what order they were in	3s 10d
1759	To examining the Engines and leather pipes	3s 0d
1765	For twice scraping and oyling the nutts, screws and works of the Engines	2s 6d

The Town Constables' role was wider than procuring and maintaining fire fighting equipment. Parliament had imposed on them a duty to attend fires; to assist in putting them out; to obtain volunteers to work the engines; to ensure that the flames did not spread; and to prevent looting.

The fire fighting abilities of these early engines were extremely limited and they would be supplemented where possible by a human conveyor belt of buckets from some nearby open water. In addition, householders were required to place a container full of water outside their front doors so that an early attack could be made on any fire. At intervals the inhabitants would be reminded of their responsibilities in this respect, as in 1712 when the town crier, John Henty, was paid fourpence 'for giveing notice to set water att door'

Added to the town inventory in 1783 was: 'One New Fire Engine with a Sucksion pipe and 40 Feet of Leather Hose (Raised by Subscription by the said James Hutchins and Richard Comber) Who also made themselves Accountable for One More Fire Engine of Equal Size and as before described.'

One of the two manual engines built by Bristow and added to the town's inventory in 1783

These were Newsham-type engines built by Bristow, of Ratcliff Highway, London Fields, a well-known manufacturer of fire fighting apparatus. One of them, polished and painted, can be seen in Anne of Cleves Museum in Southover High Street.

There was not room for these new and larger engines in the old town hall and an engine house was built for them a year later 'on a Spot of ground nigh to the Castle Gateway belonging to T. Kemp Esq., one of the Representatives in Parliament for this Borough, at his Expence, and by him presented to the Town for the aforementioned purpose.'

When the Chief Officers William Lee and John Baker handed the town's property to their successors in office in 1800 among the items listed was the engine house and three keys to it 'one to be kept by each Constable and one by Mr Durrant now occupying the Corner

House, nigh to the above premises. . . not yet been conveyed to the Town, owing more to the negligence of the Constables rather than the Disinclination of Mr Kemp, who, on our Application to him for that purposes, expressed his readiness to do it at any Time, but he has scarcely been in the country since.'

Thomas Kemp died before the situation could be formalised. The Constables continued to hand over the keys of the 'Engine House situate on the west side of Castlegate Street' to their successors in office until the autumn of 1816. Then it was discovered that, while Thomas Kemp's son, Thomas Read Kemp, was having a chapel built in his stableyard, alterations to a wall and the roof of the engine house had caused dust and mortar to fall on the engines and pipes 'as to render them incapable of Service in Case of Fire.'

The Constables at once wrote saying the property belonged to the town and what was Mr Kemp doing making alterations to it without permission. Thomas Read Kemp replied to the effect that he had always considered the building exclusively his property and he would do to it what he liked. He did add that he would direct 'any Damage done to the Engines by the alterations' to be repaired.

After some twelve months of wrangling the matter was settled. Mr Kemp came up with a counter-proposal to the Constables demand for him to complete a Deed of Gift in respect of the engine

house. He offered to erect another building for the fire appliances at his own expense in his own stableyard, or give the town £50 towards a new building elsewhere.

The town chose the latter option and in October 1818 the new Fire Engine House and Record Room (left) had been built in Fisher Street at a cost of £292. It housed the engines until 1891, when the Star Inn was

An improved horse drawn manual, seen here outside the North Street fire station, was bought in 1843. The sailor type hats worn by the crew would not have given them much protection when fighting a fire.

converted into the town hall.

Fire brigades were formed by insurance companies in London in the early eighteenth century to give greater protection to the properties the insurers had at risk than that provided by the haphazard fire fighting service of the public authorities. The companies let it be known that they had 'servants in livery, with badges, who are watermen and other lusty persons who are always to be ready when any sudden fire happens. . .'

They were not unaware of the publicity value of their fire brigades and equipped them – in London recruited mainly from Thames watermen – with resplendent uniforms. The crews were issued with large gilt or silver badges which were worn high up on the left arm. These bore the company's insignia, as did the firemarks which were placed on the front of a house as soon as a policy was taken out and the premium paid. If the burning or threatened building did not bear its company's mark, a brigade would either return to its station or remain and jeer at, and comment critically, on the performance of another company's brigade. It was not unusual for fights to break out between rival brigades while the fire blazed on unchecked.

The insurance brigades spread throughout the country but only to the large towns. They did not operate in Lewes although there are at least two firemarks here – one at 76 High Street and a second at 10 Keere Street, the old Britannia Inn – and the responsibility for fire fighting remained with the Town Constables.

However, insurance companies with offices in the town did make contributions towards the purchase of fire fighting equipment. In 1828 the British, the Sun and the Norwich Union each subscribed £5 towards the purchase of eighty feet of engine hose and four new buckets because 'the annual rate levied to defray the constables' expenses incurred during their year in office was small and sufficient only to cover costs of maintaining the engines, hoses etc.'

More companies put their hands in their pockets fourteen years later. Then the Sun, the British, the Phoenix and the Atlas each contributed £5, the Farmers gave £2 and the Protestant Defender £2 for new fire equipment.

2 THE LEWES FIRE ESTABLISHMENT

IT was decided in 1841, by Officers of the Borough, that it would be 'highly expedient' to form a Fire Establishment. A committee was set up for the purpose and serving on it were the current Constables and Headboroughs, the previous year's occupants of those offices, and agents of insurance companies from which contributions were expected.

Matters were taken several steps further when the committee of the Lewes Fire Establishment met on April 29, 1842. It decided that the new brigade should consist of two directors and twenty men; that the men, when on duty, should wear a brass badge on their right arm inscribed with the word `Fireman' and a number; that each engine be under the care of one director and ten men, whose names and places of abode should be fixed in front of the engine house; and that in the case of fire, the market bell should be rung by the bell-ringer.

These and a number of other requirements were set out in the Rules and Regulations of the Lewes Fire Establishment. Recorded in the minutes of that meeting are the names of these first two direc-tors, William Davey and Stephen Duplock, and the names of all the twenty firemen.

No sooner had these organisational decisions been made than a disastrous fire occurred in Watergate Lane where, on May 2, 1842, the entire premises and the equipment of Lee's printing works were destroyed. The fire was discovered early in the morning, when it had obtained a fierce hold in the building which housed the long established *Sussex Advertiser and Lewes Journal.*

The public water supply had been in existence for only a few years and it was the practice to shut it off each night to restrict the loss of water – something that occurred regularly in the early days. The delay in turning on the water no doubt contributed to the speed with which the fire spread. The two manual fire engines, both nearly sixty years old, were quite unequal to the task and the fire was only prevented from getting completely out of control by the speedy demolition of some wooden buildings.

The seriousness of the fire and the damage it did to the appliances can be assessed from these entries in the Town Book:

Cash paid to 158 individuals who assisted
in conveying water and working engines
at Messrs Lees' fire   £19 14s 6d
Mr W Davey's bill for repairs to engine,
new hose, standpipes   £27 12s 3d
Mr Duplock's bill for repairs of engine   £5   6s 3d

This expenditure was met from 'cash collected of the inhabitants to reward the men who assisted at Mr Lee's fire' and £152 16s 0d was contributed by people in the town, and some insurance companies, towards the cost of a new fire engine.

Although the first steam fire engine was produced in this country in 1829, steamers were not in general use until the 1860s so Lewes's new engine was an improved manual model manufactured by W J Tilley, a company which in 1851 became Shand Mason – a famous manufacturer of steamers. The new engine, which was to serve Lewes for nearly sixty years, cost less than £150 and was delivered in May 1843.

The Cliffe, which in those days was outside the borough boundary and administered separately, could call on the Lewes Fire Establishment when it needed to do so. Its own Volunteer Fire Brigade was formed in 1864 and consisted of a captain, a lieutenant, an engineer and seventeen firemen. It operated from an engine house in what was then the Fair Place and is now Cliffe Square at the sides and rear of St Thomas a Becket Church. The building is still there. It is now used as business premises and has, in recent years, acquired a stained glass fanlight with a pattern of bright red flames leaping upwards above its main entry doors.

The Cliffe brigade was launched and supported by voluntary contributions which helped to pay for its first fire engine. It was a manual one, similar to that of the Lewes brigade, and cost £120. Also like Lewes, the Cliffe brigade had its own set of rules, and they

The Cliffe Volunteer Fire Brigade with the Merryweather appliance bought for £120 and, below, the engine house in Cliffe Square, looking rather the worse for wear in the 1960s

This is Cliffe's 'beautiful new engine' which was so badly damaged in the fire at Broad's Candle Factory.

included a residential qualification for its volunteers.

There were a number of serious fires in Lewes around this time and they resulted in a further reorganisation of the town's brigade. The first was at Broad's Candle Factory in Market Street. A combination of circumstances – the inflammable nature of the contents, the length of time it took the brigade to reach the scene and difficulty in locating the hydrant – meant that the building was quickly gutted. The intense heat, thick smoke and fear of the fire spreading caused people to flee from the surrounding houses clutching as many of their possessions as they could carry.

A message calling for assistance from the Brighton Fire Brigade was dispatched. When later it was found that help would not be needed, a further message was taken by a rider on a horse from the Black Horse racing stables. He did the journey in fifteen minutes and arrived just in time to stop the departure of the Brighton appliance

The old Lewes Borough Fire Brigade, under its Captain, William Duplock, outside the White Hart Shades in Fisher Street. (Photo: Edward Reeves)

A newspaper report of the fire said the Cliffe Volunteer Fire Brigade's 'beautiful new engine was considerably damaged and rendered incapable of any further assistance when an external wall collapsed into the road.'

The second fire occurred some four months later at Elmsleys' Brewery in Malling Street. In spite of the Cliffe brigade's efforts to contain it, the building was razed to the ground. The Lewes engine had been hauled to the scene of the fire but could not be used because of a lack of water.

In 1867 the borough brigade was reformed as the Lewes Volunteer Fire Brigade. William Duplock was appointed superintendent and once more appeals went out to the townspeople and to the insurance companies for money for new hose, uniforms and helmets.

3 THE HIGHWAYS AND WORKS COMMITTEE

LEWES officially became a borough in 1881 and the responsibility for the fire brigade was given to the Highways and Works Committee of the new Corporation. The fire engines and fire brigade material which had hitherto belonged to the Constables of Lewes, on behalf of the inhabitants, were handed over to the new authority and it was no longer their right to appoint the Captain of the Fire Brigade.

The transfer is recorded in the Town Book in these words: 'We are ready to hand over all property connected with the Fire Brigade to the Corporation as the newly constituted Authority. . . and trust the efficiency of the Brigade will be continued as satisfactorily as it has been under Captain Duplock for the last twenty five years and we have reason to believe that he is willing to continue his service in that capacity'.

Under the Charter of Incorporation the boundaries of the borough were re-defined to include the Cliffe, so the new Borough of Lewes had two fire stations under its control. However, it appears that for a number of years the two stations continued to retain their separate character as two volunteer brigades.

William Duplock was appointed Superintendent of the old Lewes Borough fire engine for a period of twelve months, and Major Thomas Chatfield was appointed Chief Officer of the Cliffe brigade. When Duplock resigned his appointment, which he did in 1884, his annual report shows that the borough brigade attended six fires in twelve months. In one of them the firefighters were bedevilled by the constantly recurring problem of poor water pressure caused by the too small mains. Although the engines were at work in reasonable time, the amount of water they could direct onto the flames was so inadequate that in the space of two hours the premises, which were used as a furniture store, were completely gutted. The 1,500 people at the scene did all that they could to help the firemen and workers from the nearby Phoenix Iron Works formed a bucket chain to bring water from the river in an attempt to save the building.

Frank Davey was appointed to succeed William Duplock. Apparently the relationship between the Borough and the Cliffe was a somewhat uneasy one and it was not until 1885 that the committee resolved to 'request the Captains of the two brigades to propose within two months for approval of the Council, a gentleman who is willing to undertake the duties of Superintendent'.

In 1886 Frank Davey resigned, James Pelling was appointed Superintendent of the Borough Volunteer Fire Brigade, and the first of the Bear Yard's fires occurred.

It started in a carpenter's shop and affected both ground and first floors, burning out Strickland's corn store and stable and spreading to an adjacent house. Fire fighting operations took six hours and it was not until Brighton's steamer turned up, called by telegram, that the fire was brought under control. On this occasion lack of water could not be blamed for the Borough brigade's failure to control the fire as the river was running high and provided a plentiful supply of water.

In addition to the horse-drawn manual appliance, bought in 1843, the brigade still had its 100 year old manual. A new engine was needed urgently, but although the Highways and Works Committee asked for a trial of a Merryweather steamer in July 1887, members decided they could not 'entertain the question of purchase.'

Thomas Chatfield, the brigade's first Chief Officer, resigned his appointment in 1889. Shortly afterwards a motion instructing the Highways and Works Committee to consider the advisability of Lewes having a paid fire brigade was defeated at a special meeting of the borough council and James Pelling was promoted to fill the Chief Officer vacancy. He was only in the job a short time when, to to do away with sectional differences, he decided that the two fire stations should be numbered. Fisher Street became No 1 Station, Cliffe Square No 2 Station, and the engines were numbered accordingly.

During the next twelve months, an offer by an anonymous donor of £100 towards the purchase of a steam fire engine was not followed up, nor was a suggestion that a telephone link should be set up between the heads of the fire brigade.

In November 1891 the old Records Room and Fire Engine House in Fisher Street was demolished as part of the conversion of the Star Inn into the town hall and the fire engine moved to the back of the council chamber, which at that time was in the market hall. So, until 1906 when the North Street fire station was built, the market hall was Fire Station No 1.

James Pelling resigned on medical advice in 1895 after an association of nearly thirty years with the Lewes brigade. He was succeeded by his No 2, George Davey, a boot and shoemaker and the third Davey to lead the Lewes Fire Brigade. His reign as Chief Officer was as uneventful as was that of his predecessor.

In 1897 David Roberts, then aged 31 and Surveyor for Ashbourne Urban District Council in Derbyshire, was appointed Surveyor to Lewes Borough Council. Nine years later he also became Chief Officer of the fire brigade and under his direction it made tremendous strides.

George Davey resigned as Chief Officer in 1902 on `account of advancing years' and was succeeded by his deputy, William Parker. One cannot help feeling sorry for Parker. His No 1 Fire Station was an adapted building then more than 100 years old. His No 2 Station was little more than a shed. One of his fire engines was forty years old and his most recent acquisition, another manual bought while Davey was Chief Officer, was obsolete. Sometime, somewhere, something had to go badly wrong – and it did – at the Dusart's fire in 1904. . .

Dusart's premises in the High Street and, below, after the fire.
Photo: Edward Reeves.

4 DUSART'S FIRE

LEWES Fire Brigade's obsolete appliances were quite unable to cope with a disastrous fire at 89 High Street on October 4, 1904. The whole of Dusart's premises, which housed a hairdressing establishment offering hot and cold baths, a perfumery and a tobacconists, was ablaze and the heat was so intense that it cracked the plate glass window of Edward Reeves's photographer's shop on the opposite side of the road. And, it was said, the flint walls of St Michael's Church became too hot to touch.

Not until reinforcements in the shape of the Brighton Borough Police Brigade's new motor-driven engine and the horse-drawn steamer and manual engines of the Brighton Volunteer Fire Brigade arrived was the fire brought under control.

The Borough Council's neglect of the fire service and its reluctance to spend money when it could count on financial contributions from the fire insurance offices and from the local residents was all too obvious and it was fiercely criticised by both press and public. Everyone was well aware that without help from the Brighton brigades the devastation might have been as widespread as when the 'grete fyre was yn Westowte' in 1559.

The Dusart disaster provoked a flurry of activity. Two market-leading manufacturers of fire engines, Merryweather and Sons, and Shand Mason and Company, were asked to give competitive demonstrations of their steam fire engines. Regrettably these were horse- drawn appliances rather than the motor driven fire engines which the Brighton Borough Police Brigade had used so effectively on October 4. Money no doubt played a considerable part in the decision to opt for a horse-drawn steamer instead of a motor fire engine which would have cost at least £850.

In December 1904 responsibility for the fire brigade in Lewes passed to a new Fire Brigades Committee and it decided to buy a horse-drawn Merryweather Gem steamer at a cost of £295. The new committee also asked the borough surveyor to prepare plans and get estimates for a new fire station, stables and two cottages to

The new Merryweather Gem steamer bought in 1905 for £295 and, below, the same engine with steam up at the top of School Hill where the war memorial now stands.

be built at the Corporation Wharf, facing up North Street. To cover the cost of both the steamer and the new fire station, the council raised a loan.

It was at this juncture that Borough Surveyor David Roberts was asked to take on the duties of Chief Fire Officer for a period of twelve months to complete the modernisation of the brigade. Matters moved quickly and by 1907 the steamer and the manual were stationed at the new Engine House in North Street, fire ladders had been placed at strategic points around the town and it was decided to 'exchange Fire Engine No.2 for an escape of the latest type'.

Engine No.2 was presumably the manual purchased in 1865 by the former Cliffe Volunteer Fire Brigade. In the event the escape ladder did not materialise and the old engine was exchanged by Shand Mason and Company for a rubber-tyred hose cart.

In the years leading up to the first world war the brigade's steamer and manual engine were still pulled to fires by horses belonging to the borough council and used for a variety of purposes including pulling the rubbish carts.

This led on occasions to delayed turnouts. The steamer's crew had to wait for twenty minutes for the horses to be brought in from out of town before it could be driven to a fire at Elphick's premises in Soap Factory Lane. By the time it arrived the flames, fed by the contents of kegs of molasses soaking into bales of hay, had got a firm hold.

There were often times when firemen on foot would be at the scene of an outbreak well before the engines turned up. But it was a quick thinking and quick acting police officer who rescued the proprietor of Smiths, General Furnishers and Photographers, when this High Street shop just below Castlegate House, caught fire in 1907.

Police Constable Adams was on patrol in Castleditch Lane when he smelt smoke from the rear of the premises. He found a ladder, used it to climb into the building and rescue Mr Smith, then went to collect a hose cart from the fire station, which in those day was behind the Crown Hotel. He was back at the fire with the hose when the steamer turned up.

Quick action by Fireman Fuller prevented a fire at Thompsons

Prompt action by a police officer saved the owner when fire destroyed Smith's Furnishers in the High Street. Photo: Edward Reeves.

The Lewes brigade, called by telegram, was at the scene of the fire that gutted Cooksbridge Brewery for twelve hours in 1912.

The attendance of the steamer at the fire which burnt out Elphick's store in Soap Factory Lane was delayed for twenty minutes. The horses needed to pull it were out of town on other council business. David Roberts is on the far left, wearing epaulettes and with silver braid on his peaked cap.

drapers' shop in 1911 spreading to adjoining premises in Cliffe High Street. He grabbed a hose reel from the Cliffe fire station and had a jet of water playing on the flames just five minutes after the fire was discovered and before the brigade turned up. Cliffe residents and traders expressed their gratitude by organising a collection for him.

Another instance of the zeal of the firemen of Lewes is revealed in the following extract from an account in the *Sussex Express and County Herald* of a call out to the Rev Granville Ramage's house in Grange Road:

'Firemen Geering thought to remove the fire escape at the top of School Hill to the scene of the fire. He obtained the help of a police officer on duty and was at the top of Station Street when Chief Officer Roberts arrived on his bicycle.

'The three proceeded to guide the escape down Station Street but the steep gradient gave such impetus to the escape that it overpowered them. They hung on desperately however, the escape gathering momentum as it neared the foot of the hill. The constable had the unpleasant experience of having the sole of one of his boots ripped away in his strenuous endeavours to regain control of the escape.

'The bottom of the hill was reached at breakneck speed and by some fortunate manoeuvre those hanging on succeeded in swinging the structure round to the right and avoided crashing into the New Station Inn immediately in front of them. This difficulty being overcome, they proceeded on their way to the Manse, being overtaken near the Grange by the fire engine. . .'

5 THE BEAR HOTEL FIRE

High Street Cliffe Lewes. 581.

WHAT was described by the *Sussex Express and County Herald* as 'the most destructive fire that has taken place in Lewes and the district, at all events within living memory,' occurred early on the morning of June 18, 1918. The Bear Hotel, a 300 year old building belonging to the Southdown and East Grinstead Breweries, was totally destroyed and granaries and stores on both sides of the river were extensively damaged.

The fire was discovered at 3.40am by a shunter working in the goods yard and the Lewes brigade was quickly alerted and was on the scene within fifteen minutes. By this time the garage at the back of the hotel was burning like a furnace and the fire had reached the hotel itself on one side and a large granary belonging to Stricklands at the other. The situation was so threatening that Chief Officer David Roberts, after consultation with the mayor, called for help from Brighton, Brighton Railway and Newhaven Marine brigades.

In the meantime, the Lewes brigade continued its uphill task, its chief concern being to confine the flames to the river side of the Bear Hotel. How well they succeeded is shown by the fact that Rice Brothers cycle store caught fire eight times, the flames being

The last hours of the Bear Hotel. The cause of the fire that destroyed this fine old riverside building was never discovered.

extinguished on each occasion before the fire really caught hold.

The Bear Hotel and its contents burnt furiously and the flames gradually gained a firm hold on the granary on the other side of the garage. The blaze was so fierce that the shingled turret of the Tabernacle Sunday School hall eighty yards away on the opposite side of the river caught fire, either from a spark or from the heat. Acting Superintendent Charles Kent managed to save the building by mounting the escape with a hose and, with difficulty, climbing on to the burning roof.

Minutes later a spark from the burning buildings reached a canvas advertisement sign attached to Stevenson's warehouse, setting it on fire. The flames soon spread to the hay and straw stored inside the premises and here the heat was so great that the iron columns supporting the four storeys were melted.

The Lewes Fire Brigade was committed to preventing the spread of fire on the Cliffe side of the river and was almost powerless to deal with the extension of the fire to the opposite side of the Ouse.

The Newhaven Marine Fire Brigade travelled up the river on the tug *Hauler*. It was low tide and the *Hauler* grounded twice on its

journey upstream, finally coming to rest 200 yards short of the scene of the fire, opposite Lewes Gas Works. However, the brigade managed to run out hose over four barges and get to work with four jets.

Brighton Fire Brigade, under Superintendent La Croix, arrived on the scene with its motor fire engine when the fire was at its height. By 5am its crew had connected hose to a hydrant at the foot of School Hill and was tackling burning buildings on the town side of the river.

The Brighton Railway Fire Brigade, under Captain Glendenning, came with its engine on the 6.20am train from Brighton. This appliance, one of the most powerful in the country and capable of pumping 700 gallons a minute, added four powerful jets of water drawn from the river. By 8.30am the combined efforts of the four brigades had brought the fire under control although it was not entirely extinguished until midday.

The cause was never established.

6 BETWEEN THE WARS

AFTER a demonstration in 1922 by Dennis Brothers of Guildford an order was placed for one of the firm's 35hp motor fire engines. It cost £1,200, had solid rubber tyres and an open Braidwood body which meant that the crew was exposed to the elements.

In 1926 the brigade's rules and regulations were revised for the first time since 1905. There were new procedures in regard to attendance at fires – for instance on the receipt of a fire alarm, the engineer and driver were to proceed immediately with the engine to the fire, leaving a message on a slate in the engine house saying where they had gone.

When the engine went outside the borough, the rules required two firefighters and a messenger to be detailed to remain on duty at the fire station during the time the engine was away. They also listed the

The brigade's first Dennis pump behind a National Benzole tanker containing 800 gallons of fuel, the cab of which caught fire at Hope in the Valley in 1927.

Lewes Borough Fire Brigade in 1919, with Chief Officer David Roberts (seated centre) and, below, members of the Fire Brigade Committee in The Paddock to see a drill display and to inspect the brigade.

punishments for various derelictions of duty. A firefighter turning up drunk faced instant dismissal. The wilful neglect or refusal to attend a fire when called incurred a fine of ten shillings, as did leaving the scene of a fire, except if injured or with permission of the officer in charge.

The new rules showed for the first time some concern for the welfare of the firefighters. At fires of long duration, the officer in charge was expected to 'determine the nature of any refreshment required and the time when it should be allowed.'

David Roberts resigned because of poor health in 1929 after more than twenty three years as Chief Fire Officer. The borough council placed on record its 'high appreciation' of his unstinted services in the cause of fire prevention and of his great ability in the organisation and leadership of the Lewes Fire Brigade of which he was made an honorary Chief Officer. He was succeeded by George Carter, who had been the brigade's Superintendent since 1917 and had served with it for twenty two years,

The Fire Brigade Committee was now concerned not just with the extinction of fires but with fire prevention. It discussed matters such as the testing of fire appliances in cinemas and other public buildings as well as expressing views and inspecting plans, at the request of the Sanitary Committee, in connection with the granting of licences to store petrol.

A second Dennis fire engine was purchased in 1934 at a cost of £1,312. Like the earlier Dennis pump, this also had an open Braidwood body but ran on pneumatic tyres rather than solid ones. Its equipment included a fifty feet wheeled escape, a 120 feet hose reel which operated from a forty gallon water tank and a powerful pump which had a capacity of more than 400 gallons per minute. The old horse-drawn manual engine was sold for £5 to the Glynde Estate – to be used for fire drill practice by the estate workers.

By now the fire brigade had begun to assume a wider role than that of putting out fires. The records for 1937, for instance, show that its equipment and pumps were deployed to deal with pumping out flooded cellars at the Castle Inn and the Thatched House public house in South Street.

It was also called to deal with an unusual incident on March 16 of that year. The barge *Shamrock* had jammed under Cliffe bridge and the brigade had to pump sixty tons of water into its hold in order to lower the height of the vessel in the water and so free it.

The barge *Shamrock* with her bows well and truly stuck under Cliffe bridge.

It was after this demonstration outside Barbican House that the decision was taken in 1922 to buy a Dennis 35hp motor pump.

The Dennis pump with open Braidwood body bought in 1934 and, below,
Chief Officer George Carter and Engineer Freddie Geering receiving
awards for their part in a rescue during a fire at 11 Market Street.

7 THE AFS AND THE NFS

IN 1939 the Auxiliary Fire Service (AFS) was created. Those local authorities, who were also fire brigade authorities, were required to draw up fire brigade organisation schemes and to submit their requirements for extra equipment to the Home Office.

Lewes Borough Council formed a permanent sub-committee to deal with Air Raid Precaution matters of a technical nature. It was made up of elected members, officers of the council including the Chief Fire Officer, and representatives of the gas and electric light companies, as well as the post office telephones.

A further piece of legislation, the Fire Brigades Act of 1938, made it mandatory for all local authorities, except county councils, to establish and maintain an efficient fire service and local authorities were given until April 1940 to implement its provisions.

The effect of this legislation was that Chailey Rural District Council formed its own fire brigade with stations at Barcombe, Ditchling, Peacehaven and, to cover neighbouring villages, at Lewes. Chailey Rural District Council's Lewes Station operated from premises in St Nicholas Lane and Clifford Geering, the former second engineer of the Lewes Fire Brigade was appointed Lewes District Fire Officer.

By 1940 a number of strategically placed auxiliary or action stations had been set up around the town. They were staffed by Auxiliary Fire Service personnel and generally equipped with a towing vehicle and a light trailer pump.

In Lewes they were sited in the garages of Shelleys Hotel, the De Warenne Road Stores, the Market Tower in Market Street, the Cliffe Volunteer Fire Brigade's engine house in Cliffe Square, in premises which are now Gorringe's Auction Rooms in North Street, in the old chapel on Chapel Hill and in a cow shed attached to Saxonbury, a house in Kingston Road, Southover. This last one was moved in 1940 to the Elm Tree Stables, Southover.

Largely as a result of experiences in the London blitz, when voluntary fire watchers saved St Paul's Cathedral from destruction by dealing immediately with the incendiary bombs that fell on it, a Statutory Order was made in January 1941 requiring the presence of fire watching parties in industrial and commercial premises.

Shortly after the introduction of this Order, the East Sussex Steam Laundry's premises in Malling Street were destroyed by fire. The Town Clerk summoned the Steam Laundry Company for failing to ensure that the person who had undertaken to act as a fire watcher was at all necessary times present on the premises on the night in question – January 17, 1941. The case was dismissed by the magistrates.

The heavy air raids on provincial cities and the attempts to provide mutual assistance had shown that not only were tbe fire-fighting resources provided by the existing fire authorities inadequate in such testing conditions but that a far greater degree of co-ordination, organisation and standardisation was required.

Accordingly the Government decided to nationalise the country's fire services and on August 18, 1941 the National Fire Service was formed. The AFS was absorbed into the new organisation and many of the temporary fire stations abandoned.

Under the National Fire Service, England and Wales were divided into thirty three fire areas each under the control of a Fire Force Commander. These fire areas varied in size, but they usually included two or more counties and all the fire brigades in an area were combined to form a single Fire Force.

Lewes fell within Fire Force Area 31, which covered Sussex and parts of Kent and Surrey and was commanded by Charles Birch, the Chief Fire Officer of Brighton. It was divided into four divisions based on Brighton, Hassocks, Tunbridge Wells and Bexhill.

In Lewes itself there were three fire stations. Station 31 BX was in premises which now no longer exist – the Elm Tree Stables in Southover; Station 31 BY, originally at the old Cliffe Fire Station, but from 1942 in converted premises in Malling Street; and Station 31 BZ at the old fire station in North Street.

Later in 1942, the Regional Commitee directed that the Fire (Residential Buildings) Order should apply to Lewes. This required

NFS Company Officer Leslie Brown, Divisional Officer Arthur Bowles and Column Officer Neville Mountford.

that not less than four gallons of water in a portable container or containers, which could be readily used with a stirrup pump, should be placed immediately inside or outside the main door of a building – for Lewes householders a revival of an eighteenth century custom.

There had been no casualties and only light damage in Lewes as a result of air raids until January 20, 1943 when enemy fighter bombers dropped six high explosive bombs as well as attacking the town with machine gun and cannon fire. The bombs fell in Brook Street, at the top of North Street, at the junction of New Street and West Street, at the bottom of St Martin's Lane near the entrance to the railway tunnel and two on New Road. There were two fatalities.

Among the properties badly damaged in this raid was the Stag Hotel in North Street. After the fire there had been put out it flared up again and completed the destruction of the Stag. A complaint from a local resident about the way in which the NFS dealt with the incident led to an inquiry by Divisional Officer Arthur Bowles. He concluded that no blame should be attributed to any member of the fire fighting team.

Later that year, George Carter, Chief Officer of the Lewes Fire Brigade prior to the war, announced his retirement after thirty five years in the fire service.

More than 100 firefighters fought this blaze at the Phoenix Ironworks in in May 1948. It was the first large fire attended by appliances of the newly formed East Sussex Fire Brigade.

8 THE EAST SUSSEX FIRE BRIGADE

THE Government had promised that when the war was over the fire service would be handed back to local authority control. This was done on April 1, 1948. From that day responsibility for the fire service was but vested in the county and county borough councils, rather than the borough and district councils which had managed them previously. This meant that the provision of a fire service in Lewes became the responsibility of the East Sussex County Council and the fire station in North Street became Station 1, East Sussex Fire Brigade.

Agreement was reached on the acquisition and development of land at the rear of the fire station, to provide a drill tower and training ground at a capital cost of £15,000. Moves were also made to acquire adjoining land owned by Shell Mex.

The new organisation had an early and severe test on May 19. What was to be the most serious fire for many years started in the pattern shop of Every's Phoenix Ironworks and quickly vented through the roof. Soon the whole central block went up in flames and was totally destroyed and sparks were blown on to the roof of the old Naval Prison, but were extinguished.

To compound the problem there were four other fires in the county at the same time and Lewes's water tender had been moved to Crowborough to provide cover there because stations in that area had been denuded of appliances.

Retained personnel had been called in to standby at Lewes and it was they who responded to the call from Every's, with additional firemen coming in to crew the second appliance when the siren sounded. At the height of the fire nearly 100 firefighters from Lewes, Keymer, Seaford, Newhaven and Barcombe were involved.

The year ended with an agreement in principle to the installation in 1950/51 of a wireless communications scheme for the twenty five stations in the county brigade.

In the twelve month period to the end of March 1950, crews from

In historic towns like Lewes, with many old buildings packed together, there is always the fear of a blaze spreading throughout a block. In all fifteen appliances and ninety men from ten stations were needed to contain the outbreak at Baxter's Printing Works in 1955.

Lewes Fire Station attended a total of 180 calls – a number not equalled again for more than twenty years. There were eighty nine calls to fires, thirty one to chimney fires, ten false alarms, twenty three special service calls and twenty seven occasions when assistance was rendered to other stations.

In common with other fire services from all over the country East Sussex Fire Brigade was involved in disaster limitation work following the East Coast floods in February 1953 in which 280 people lost their lives. It sent ten pumping appliances and sixty four firemen, including several from Lewes, to Whitstable in Kent.

Later that year the old Lewes Fire Brigade's second Dennis pump NJ 2949, acquired in 1934 was scrapped and its spare parts used to keep other Dennis appliances running.

The largest fire since Every's Phoenix Ironworks conflagration some seven years previously, was on September 15, 1955 at Baxter's Printing Works in the High Street. Two appliances from Lewes fire station responded to the call and Station Officer Bill Izzard found a severe fire and volumes of dense smoke in the rear of the premises in St Nicholas Lane, used for packing and for storing paper.

It was clear the situation was dangerous and a wireless message was sent to brigade control for four more pumps. The fire continued to spread rapidly and it seemed likely that the whole block would soon be ablaze. More pumps were called for and, after much exhausting work, often under difficult and arduous conditions, the fire was gradually surrounded and brought under control.

In all fifteen appliances and ninety firefighters from ten stations attended this outbreak. Much of their efforts went into preventing the spread of fire to adjacent buildings such as the Dolphin public house in St Nicholas Lane, and a county council building in Walwers Lane which, although separated from Baxter's premises by a six feet wide passage, was damaged by radiated heat.

The number of calls attended by Lewes in 1959/60 was 177, of which 108 were to fires, twenty five to chimney fires, twenty two false alarms, twenty special services calls and two calls to assist other brigades.

A Green Goddess at work at Lewes railway station where, at the height of the floods, water reached platform height above the track.

In November 1960 it was the turn of the Lewes area to be flooded, not, as on the east coast from high seas and hurricane winds, but from heavy rain and melting snow. The fifty seven special services rendered by the brigade included rescuing people and cattle marooned by the flood water, salvaging furniture and pumping out homes, shops and offices.

Three large Civil Defence appliances pumped almost continuously for forty five hours at Hoopers Lane, assisting River Board pumps to lower the level of flood water in that part of Lewes, while another large emergency pump, mounted on a truck at the railway station, worked continuously for sixty hours. Even the North Street fire station itself was flooded and the fire brigade had to be evacuated to the part of the old Naval Prison grounds used by Civil Defence.

Perhaps it was coincidence but when the waters subsided it was decided to include in the capital programme for 1968/69 the provision of a new fire station in North Street, together with a brigade stores building.

Two pumping appliances from Lewes were among the twelve

pumps, three turntable ladders, and one breathing apparatus tender mobilised to the fire that devastated Hove Town Hall in 1966. The main hall of the building was gutted, the council chamber, magistrates court, committee rooms and offices in the east wing either burnt out or severely damaged and the roof and part of the second floor in the west wing also badly damaged.

A fire at Lewes Prison two years later could have had fatal consequences, had it not been for the action of a prison officer and two prisoners. They rescued members of a search crew whose air supply was not sufficient to sustain them in the fume-filled basement where large quantities of plastic materials were stored. The firefighters were unaware of this hazard as local authority brigades had no statutory rights of inspection of Crown Property to advise on fire safety.

After studying the Chief Fire Officer's report of the prison fire the county council supported the view that brigade should have such a facility but, after hearing the views of Her Majesty's Inspector of Fire Brigades, it decided not to make representations to the Association

Aftermath of a fire. The remains of the great hall of Hove Town Hall .

of County Councils on the matter.

Bill Izzard was awarded the British Empire Medal in the1969 New Year's Honours List and he was succeeded at Lewes by Dennis Stebbings. By the end of the year the brigade's programme for the changeover from oxygen breathing apparatus sets to compressed air had been completed and a start made on replacing station sirens and house bells, used to mobilise retained firemen, by personal pagers. Other new equipment including air-powered zip guns and Epco hydraulic rescue kits – a great improvement on the earlier rescue gear.

Fire call statistics were now kept on a calendar year basis rather than from April to March like the Inland Revenue's financial year. Records for 1970 show that Lewes attended forty two fires, seventeen small fires, thirty seven chimney fires, twenty six false alarms, thirty three special service operations and fifteen assistance calls to other brigades – a total of 170 call outs.

Dennis Stebbings moved to brigade headquarters in January 1972 and was succeeded, on a temporary basis, by Mike Turner pending the appointment of Station Officer David Clark, a staff officer from brigade headquarters. In February 1973 Station Officer Tom Brown was appointed Station Commander at Lewes.

The new fire station became operational on February 1, 1972, and on May 13 it was officially opened by Lewes's MP, Sir Tufton Beamish. The tenancy of the Watch Room and other accommodation at the old fire station was offered to Lewes Borough Council for a period of two years, as well as the offices at 2 Corporation Villas. The brigade held on to the appliance room as accommodation for spare appliances.

A former signals vehicle from the disbanded Civil Defence Corps was acquired for use as a mobile control unit at large fires. The vehicle, which was to be based at the fire station, cost £90 and a further £85 had to be spent to on it so it would comply with the Motor Vehicles (Construction and Use) Regulations.

Call out records for 1972 show Lewes attended its highest number of incidents since 1950. There were 212, of which fifty five were

The new fire station, opened in May 1972 by Lewes's MP, Sir Tufton Beamish and, below, the old fire station, built in 1907 as part of the re-organisation which followed the Dusart's fire.

Freddie Geering (left) joined the fire service as a messenger in 1911, retiring fifty years later as a Retained Sub-Officer. Fireman Bill Fuller was elected Mayor of Lewes in 1974.

fires, forty nine small fires, forty two chimney fires, twenty nine false alarms, nineteen special services, eighteen assistance calls to other brigades. In addition assistance was given to other stations on twenty three occasions.

Courts furniture shop in Friars Walk was destroyed by fire in November 1973. Fifteen pumping appliances from Lewes, Newhaven, Uckfield, Burgess Hill, Haywards Heath, Barcombe, Seaford, Hove, Hurstpierpoint and Brighton were at the scene and the crews had to work under conditions of severe heat as they fought to prevent the spread of fire which was rapid, due to the close proximity of adjoining buildings and the nature of their construction.

9 LOCAL GOVERNMENT RE-ORGANISATION

ON April 1, 1974, the fire brigades of Brighton, Eastbourne, East Sussex and Hastings were merged to form the new East Sussex Fire Brigade. Its Chief Officer was Eric Whitaker, formerly Chief Fire Officer of the old East Sussex Fire Brigade.

Under the terms of the reorganisation, the East Sussex stations of Haywards Heath, East Grinstead, Burgess Hill, Turners Hill, Hurstpierpoint and Keymer became part of West Sussex Fire Brigade, while Lewes, otherwise known as Station 1, was part of East Sussex's new seven station A Division, under the command of Senior Divisional Officer Bob Clark.

The Control Unit, although based at Lewes, was mobilised to any fires in the county requiring an attendance of five or more pumping appliances. Thus Lewes firefighters saw more of the geographical county than personnel from most other stations and some of the largest fires.

The HAZCHEM Scheme, by which emergency services personnel are able to identify the steps they need to take to deal with an incident involving hazardous chemicals, was introduced nationally; as was a 48 hour working week for firemen.

Since Bill Izzard's retirement in 1969 there had been a succession of Station Commanders at Lewes, among them two from the Royal Berkshire Fire Brigade – Station Officers Jerry Beech and Roger Hayto. In 1978 Roger Hayto's successor was an internal appointee, Sub-Officer Vincent Richardson, and he was to give the fire station the continuity that it needed.

The centralisation of all 999 calls within the county was completed by the end of March 1976, from which time all fire calls were received at, and all appliances mobilised from, the control room at brigade headquarters in King Henry's Road, Lewes.

The long hot summer that followed made 1976 the busiest twelve month period in 400 years of fire-fighting in Lewes. Crews had no sooner dealt with one incident and returned to the station when, often without being able to change a soiled uniform or to have a shower, they were called out again.

Life was particularly difficult for the retained firefighters who had other employment as well as their fire brigade duties. Their dedication and that of all personnel was commended by the then Home Secretary and Labour MP, Merlyn Rees, the Minister responsible for the fire service.

'The manner in which whole-time and retained members of the Fire Service have fought the unprecedented spate of fires during the recent dry weather has deservedly earned widespread public gratitude,' he wrote. 'This has made very heavy demands upon the service and I congratulate all concerned on the way in which, in the best traditions of the Fire Service, they have responded to those demands.'

During that year Lewes attended fifty nine fires, eighty small fires, twenty eight chimney fires, thirty two false alarms and forty six special services – a total of 245 calls. In addition there were 101 occasions when they gave assistance to other stations.

The worsening financial situation in local government began to bite in the late 1970s and the Public Protection Committee approved budget savings which were to have an effect on fire protection, officer cover, administration and other areas of brigade activity. Fortunately the reductions had little impact, if any, on Lewes Fire Station and the community it served,

Pay awards which were considered inadequate, union militancy and general industrial unrest resulted in emergency calls only being answered by members of the Fire Brigade's Union for a week from September 5, 1977.

This demonstration was the prelude to the first national strike in the British Fire Service. On November 14, together with their comrades in other parts of the country, 315 whole-time and part-time personnel in the East Sussex Fire Brigade reluctantly withdrew their services. Lewes, in common with other stations where whole-time firemen were based, had no one available to answer fire calls.

The new control/canteen unit and a Dennis water tender ladder on display at Glyndebourne.

The government had planned for the emergency and Green Goddess fire appliances were brought out of mothballs and crewed by Armed Forces personnel. Initially six Green Goddesses were allocated to East Sussex. Three were based at the Territorial Army Volunteer Reserve Centre in Brighton, one at the TAVR Centre in Eastbourne and two in Hastings. Later two additional appliances were located at Lewes Prison.

Originally soldiers of the 9th Parachute Squadron (Royal Engineers) provided the county's fire cover but in December they were replaced by the 24th Field Squadron (Royal Engineers) while Royal Navy crews manned the Eastbourne appliance. The strike ended on January 16, 1978, the government having agreed a new pay formula and a reduced working week.

The old Civil Defence vehicle, used since 1972 as a control unit, was replaced by a new Bedford single deck coach with much improved canteen facilities as well as a sophisticated control and command centre. It was among the appliances, which included ten pumps and two rescue tenders called to the tragic train crash at Sweethill near Patcham tunnel, Brighton on December 19. It was able to meet all demands for food and drink throughout the many hours of this protracted incident.

A forty two hour working week was introduced in March 1979 and the full-time establishment at Lewes was increased to fourteen – a station officer, a sub-officer, three leading firefighters and nine firefighters. This was an increase of two operational personnel on its 1974 establishment. However, budget savings exercises were still going on and a few years later the hours of the station cook and the cleaner were reduced.

In 1982 Lewes responded to 241 calls, only four short of the 1976 record. The following year was only slightly less busy than with 233 incidents attended – sixty one fires, forty small fires, thirty five chimney fires, forty three false alarms, fifty three special services, one occasion when assistance was given to another brigade as well as 140 assistance calls to other stations.

10 THE BOMB EXPLOSION
AT BRIGHTON

ON October 12, 1984, firemen from Lewes were involved in what was probably the most dramatic incident in the history of the town's Fire Service – the bomb explosion at the Grand Hotel, Brighton.

The media was there to cover the Conservative Party conference and, as a result, the protracted and often dangerous rescue operations were carried out in the full glare of publicity.

The original call was received and logged at Brigade Control at 02.54 hours and the normal predetermined attendance of pump escape, water tender and turntable ladder from Preston Circus Fire Station was mobilised. The officer in charge of the first attendance, Station Officer Fred Bishop, found the explosion had caused severe damage to the centre front section of all floors, with the most serious damage at fifth, sixth and seventh floor levels.

Once he had issued initial instructions to his crews he called for reinforcing appliances, confirming that although an explosion had taken place, the building was not on fire. After an extensive tour of the wrecked building, Station Officer Bishop informed Brigade Control that upwards of 270 people were still unaccounted for. Seventeen minutes after the initial call, eight pumping appliances, two turntable ladders and an hydraulic platform were either in attendance or responding to the incident.

Once the initial and obvious rescues had taken place and the premises evacuated, fire service personnel, including crews from Lewes, entered the worst affected areas of the building on the upper floors. Rescue squads were formed under the command of designated officers and various rescue operations began to proceed simultaneously, while efforts to determine the number of people actually trapped in the debris continued. Throughout the incident, and particularly in the early stages, the possibility of further explosive devices in the building could not be discounted and this added another dimension of danger to the problems that had to be faced. There were many individual examples of courage and total commitment to the difficult task of search and rescue by all members of the Fire Service from both East and West Sussex.

When it had been determined that only two people were still missing, the size of operations was scaled down and appliances retained at the scene only as necessary. The last body was removed by the brigade at 01.33 hours on October 13. One further body was recovered by the Bomb Squad nearly twenty four hours later. In all twelve people were rescued, or bodies recovered, with Fire Brigade assistance.

The Prime Minister, Mrs Margaret Thatcher, expressed her personal appreciation of the Fire Service's action in a letter to Eric Whitaker, Chief Fire Officer at Lewes. It reads:

'The speed of response, the skill of operation and, above all, the magnificent courage of the Fire Service in working in conditions of great and growing danger following the bomb explosion in Brighton has been the subject of universal admiration.

'I am writing to ask you to pass on my personal appreciation to all those involved for their devoted and selfless professionalism to which some of my closest colleagues and friends owe their lives. Just as we are saddened by the wickedness of people responsible for outrages of this sort, the example set by your men is an example and an inspiration to the nation as a whole.'

11 NOW INTO THE NINETIES

ERIC WHITAKER, Chief Fire Officer at Lewes, who had been Chief Officer of the merged brigades since 1974 and of the old East Sussex Fire Brigade for some four years before that, retired in November 1994. He was succeeded by his deputy, Peter Rodgers.

Lewes's Station Commander, Vince Richardson, retired in February 1989. Like his father before him he had given many years of unstinted service to the community of Lewes. He was succeeded by Station Officer John Ticehurst, a Watch Commander from Preston Circus Fire Station, Brighton who, a year later, moved back to Preston Circus – the busiest station in the county – as Station Commander there. Mike Rogers, another Watch Commander from Preston Circus, whose father was Chief Officer of West Sussex Fire Brigade, succeeded John Ticehurst at Lewes in 1990.

The exceptionally hot summers of 1989 and 1990 kept Lewes busier, in fact, than in the long hot summer of 1976. Turnouts totalled 492 and 458 respectively and among them was the worst fire in the county – at Malling House, the headquarters of the Sussex police, on October 4, 1990..

Brigade control, just across the river in North Street, received a call from the police at 10.39am reporting the fire. Two water tender ladders from Lewes were immediately despatched and on arrival the officer in charge saw smoke coming from a ground floor sash window and a security officer fighting the fire with an extinguisher.

Closer inspection showed that the fire had already reached the vertical cavity and was spreading rapidly to the first floor of this Georgian house with interior walls lined with wood panelling and wall and roof cavities extended throughout the structure.

The number of pumping appliances were increased to four and fire fighters wearing breathing apparatus entered the building with hose reels to attack the fire and to limit its spread. As crews fought to bring the fire under control others searched the premises and began salvage operations. The fire spread rapidly and pumping appliances were further increased to six, then to eight and finally to twelve so that more fire fighters in breathing apparatus could be deployed throughout building. A turntable ladder and a rescue tender were also needed and were provided from Preston Circus.

As the number of supporting appliances was being built up further teams entered the building to assist fire fighting operations and to continue salvage work. This sustained attack and the efforts of crews who were working under difficult and punishing conditions, eventually brought the fire under control. At the height of the conflagration sixteen sets of breathing apparatus were in use and five hose reels.

Although the fire occurred in a building well within East Sussex, the appliances attending included one from Keymer in West Sussex and a second West Sussex appliance stood by at Lewes while its own vehicles were committed to the incident.

Peter Rodgers retired as Chief Officer in 1991. He was succeeded by Peter Morphew, then Chief Fire Officer of Bedfordshire, who in 1995 moved to the Home Office as one of Her Majesty's Inspectors.

County Fire Officer Alan McCormack now leads Lewes, and the other twenty three fire stations under his command, towards an uncertain future.

Prior to the last general election, all three major political parties indicated their intention to abolish county councils which currently provide the fire service outside the metropolitan areas. The Adam Smith Institute suggested privatisation of the fire service and there were reports in the national press that the government was considering nationalising the fire service in England and Wales and running it as an executive agency. Another suggestion was that there might a fire service based on eight regions and controlled by a central body.

A Local Government Commission was appointed to look at the local government map, area by area, with a view to creating unitary authorities larger than the present district councils and reducing the number of county councils. Among its recommendations is a new unitary authority for Brighton and Hove with the remainder of East Sussex continuing with a two tier system comprising a smaller county council and five district councils.

The old Lewes fire engine station as it looks today.

In the short term this has implications for the Fire Brigade's relationship with the new unitary authority of Brighton and Hove and the provision of a fire service for that area. In the long term a pan-Sussex Fire Authority seems likely, with both the police and ambulance services also operating across the whole county.

Whatever the future of the fire service, historically the people of Lewes have been well served by their fire brigade, no matter how it has been organised and managed.

Irrespective of whether the service is nationalised or regionalised or whether the two brigades of East and West Sussex are merged, one thing is certain – Lewes's fire fighters will continue to give the people of the town the highest possible standards of service in the provision of fire cover and fire safety.

APPENDIX

THIS list of appliances is fairly comprehensive, it not definitive as undoubtedly there have been other appliances, particularly since 1948, which have been based at Lewes, albeit for relatively short periods, while its own appliances have been off the road for some reason or between disposal and purchase.

ABBREVIATIONS			
ARV	Animal Rescue Vehicte	PE	Pump Escape
CU	Control Unit	RP	Rescue Pump
GP	General or Dual Purpose	SP	Self Propelled Pump
HRU	Heavy Rescue Unit	TV	Towing Vehicle
HRV	Heavy Rescue Vehicle	WrE	Water Tender Escape
LU	Lighting Unit	WrL	Water Tender Ladder
P	Pump	WrT	Water Tender

Year	Reg. No	Make	Type	Notes
1680				Three "ingins", one great and two small.
1690				Two "ingins", one great and one small.
1726				An engine with two leather pipes given by Thomas Pelham of Lewes.
1731				An engine of smaller size given by Thomas Pelham of Stanmer.
1782				Two engines of the fourth size built by Bristow of Ratcliffe Highway, London Fields.
1843		W J Tilley		Manual appliance for Lewes Fire Establishment.
1864		Merryweather		Manual appliance made for Cliffe Volunteer Fire Brigade.
1895/1900				Further manual appliance bought.
1905		Merryweather		Gem steamer, horse-drawn.
1922		Dennis		35 hp motor appliance with solid tyres.
1934	NJ 2949	Dennis	PE	Broken up for spares, 1953.
1939	BPM 213	Dennis	SP	Transferred to Lewes November 1963, sold June 1965.

Year	Reg No.	Make	Type	Notes
1939	BPN 644	Dennis	SP	Transferred to Lewes May 1956, disposed of July 1964.
1943	GXM 609	Dodge	WrT	Disposed of January 1951.
1943	GXH 136	Austin	TV	Based at Lewes from July 1947, disposed of March 1954.
	GYR 135	Bedford	GP	Fitted with stack grab 1950, disposed of August 1952.
	GYR 760	Bedford	WrT	Transferred out March 1949, returned to Lewes April 1952, disposed of October 1955. Fitted with stack grab.
1950	FAP 534	Commer / Miles	WrT	Left Lewes February 1954, sold 1966 for £85.
1950	FNJ 703	Land Rover		Based at Lewes for four months in 1952.
1952	GNJ 793	Land Rover		Disposed of September 1961.
1953	HPM 438	Bedford/ Miles	WrE	Left Lewes 1965, sold June 1972 for £110.
1955	KAP 21	Karrier	WrT	Divisional reserve. Transferred to Lewes July 1968, disposed of 1970.
1958	UXH 698	Ford Thames	CU	Ex Civil Defence signals vehicle, acquired by brigade 1969.
1960	SNJ 318	Commer/ Carmichael	PE	Sold January 1974 for £115.
1961	TPN 450	Karrier/ Carmichael	WrT	Divisional reserve.
1961	VNJ 121	Land Rover		
1962	XPN 906	Bedford TK	WrT	Transferred fromHeathfield October 1973, sold June 1977 for £194.
1964	CPN 602B	Bedford TK/ HCB	WrT	Transferred to HGV training October 1973, sold March 1978 for £324.
1964	CPN 603B	Bedford TK/ HCB	WrT	Transferred to Bexhill sold July 1981 for £253.
1965	CPN 601B	Bedford TK/ HCB	PE	Transferred to Hove, sold August 1980 for £230.
1970	LDY 752J	Land Rover		
1970	UPM 349H	Land Rover	LU	Transferred to Crowborough,sold June 1991, for £1,363.
1970	UPM 350H	Land Rover	P	Transferred from Crowborough to Preston Circus when ARV delivered.

Year	Reg No	Make	Type	Notes
1973	KNJ 912L	Dennis	WrL	Became second machine (WrT) on delivery of BUF 993T, given to Ethiopia, September 1989
1978	LVH 196T	Bedford Coach	CU	Currently in service
1979	BUF 993T	Bedford CSV/HCB	WrL	Became second machine (WrT) on delivery of D455 XAP. Sold 1994.
1987	D455 XAP	Bedford	WrL	Currently in service as second machine.
1990	H521 YAP	Mercedes	ARV	Transferred to Newhaven for use as foam tender.in 1993.
1993	K709 LYJ	Volvo FL614/ Excalibur	RP	Currently in service.
1984	A779 EPN	Jeep	HRV	Temporarily placed at Lewes in 1994 pending delivery of purpose built Heavy Rescue Unit
1995	M128 BPN	Volvo FL614/ Bedwas	HRU	Not yet in operational use.

Bedford water tender CPN 602B, with bodywork by HCB-Angus

The Fire Service of today has many rescue roles. Here a hang glider pilot who became entangled with a power cable in Mill Lane, Rodmell on a summer Sunday in 1993 is expertly released from his dangerous predicament by firefighters from Lewes.

Photo: Evening Argus

BIBLIOGRAPHY

A History of the British Fire Service by G V Blackstone (Routledge, Kegan Paul)
A History of the Lewes Fire Service, an unpublished document by Les Davey held in the East Sussex Records Office.
East Sussex County Council:
  Minutes of the Fire Brigade Committee, 1948 to 1974.
  Minutes of the Public Protection Committee, 1974 to 1993.
  East Sussex Fire Brigade annual reports, 1948 to 1967.
Focus on Fire, East Sussex Fire Brigade house magazine.
Kelly's Directories of Lewes.
Lewes Borough Council:
  Resolution of a Meeting of Officers, 1841.
  Highways and Works Committee minutes, 1881 to 1904.
  Fire Brigade Committee minutes, 1904 to 1940.
  Civil Defence progress reports 1940 to 1941.
Lewes Fire Establishment Committee meeting, 1842.
Lewes Fire Establishment, rules and regulations.
Pike's Directories of Lewes, Newhaven and Seaford (Garrett, Mepham and Fisher).
Sussex Express and County Herald and its predecessor newspapers.
Town Books of Lewes 1542 to 1701, 1702 to 1837, 1837 to 1901 (Sussex Historical Society).
Town Constables Accounts, 1693 to 1881.
War in East Sussex (Sussex Express and County Herald)

PICTURE CREDITS

THE majority of the photographs in this book are from the archives of the East Sussex Fire Brigade. A number are from old postcards or photographs kindly lent to me by friends. Where I have been able to trace the source of a photograph it is indicated in the caption.